A
CONCEPTUAL
CIRCUS

I0619924

A
CONCEPTUAL
CIRCUS

KENNETH JARRETT SINGLETON

ARPress
ILLUMINATING IDEAS,
EMPOWERING VOICES

Copyright © 2021 by Kenneth Jarrett Singleton.

All rights reserved. No part of this publication may be reproduced, distributed, or transmitted in any form or by any means, including photocopying, recording, or other electronic or mechanical methods, without the prior written permission of the copyright owner and the publisher, except in the case of brief quotations embodied in critical reviews and certain other noncommercial uses permitted by copyright law. For permission requests, write to the publisher, addressed "Attention: Permissions Coordinator," at the address below.

ARPress
45 Dan Road Suite 5
Canton MA 02021

Hotline: 1(800) 220-7660
Fax: 1(855) 752-6001

Ordering Information:
Quantity sales. Special discounts are available on quantity purchases by corporations, associations, and others. For details, contact the publisher at the address above.

Printed in the United States of America.

ISBN-13:   Softcover   979-8-89356-956-8
           eBook   979-8-89356-957-5

Library of Congress Control Number: 2024909582

Contents

Five Poems From Exotic Neurotic

The Exercise of Abscission

Something left.
Something more.
More than you I long for gore.
Soothed in comfort by what ails them, and what will strike again.

Something right.
Something less.
The grand provider has come to bless.
Harps somehow played by the fingerless;
Those who did abstain.

Intersperse.
Inner core.
They'll try to exit with something more.
Later will come bountiful fortunes for those who leave a stain.

Madam Mize, do a reprise.
I want you to tell me lies.
Madam Mize, do surprise.
There are many things to memorize.

Mystic spells.
Parallels.
Oral moments with oral gels.
Despite her candidiasis;
So superbly sings the thrush.

Aquarelles.
Useless prayers.
Rigid trances and rigid stares.
We're enamored with the home's decor and the shape-shifting of the bust.

Hypnotized.
Hypno-state.
Suffocation inside the crate;
Such traumas should be valued, and undergone again.

Madam Mize, do abscise;
Separate the ties.
Madam Mize, it's no surprise;
The turning spectacle will mesmerize.

Former use.
Former friend;
I'm picking at it so it doesn't mend.
Long ago going with progression seemed like the thing to do.

Formulate.
Insert pins.
He'll be screaming when it begins.
Such a disservice he's done to himself;
Puncturing is due.

Faces melt.
Seldom felt;
Is the heat so adored and dealt.
Take our breath with granted humidity.
The endowment of a blistered earth.

Madam Mize, cut the ties.
Cut the ribbons from the prize.
I'm pleased with their demise;
And the gathering of flies.

Madam Mize, kindly abscise;
For amusement and what it implies.
I want to hear their cries;
From the abscission exercise.

Body Bound

I am now body bound.
Look at what I have found.
Your precious body's bound.
You, the process will confound.
You are a layman;
But I'm not putting it in simple terms.
Your lamentation.
The ones beneath share space with worms.

I am not sure just where it originated.
I'm sure you'll be happier when incarcerated.
Bound and proverbial.
You are primordial;
A primordial blessing.
I really like the way you're dressing.

A performance forming;
What a substantive gift.
You are transforming;
What a substantive lift.
Physique bound execution.
This is special to both of us.
A permanent solution.
Tactility with snugness.

I'm not so sure just how we originated.
I want you to become more incensed and adulterated.
Show me that you're worthwhile.
Let me see your lifestyle.
Do you see it's ingrained;
Fixed firmly within your mind?
Keep your hatred sustained;
Too much has happened to be kind.

I can't put a value on what I have discovered.
Flaunt your bruising for me;
Remain uncovered.
An exhibition;
Done by the precisionist.
Malnutrition;
Caused by an exhibitionist.

You look much better now;
Since the changes.
One must first take apart;
Before one rearranges.
Allow me to shape you;
It's for my personal benefit.
Ask them to rape you;
Show them all that you're legit.

Beautifully crafted.
So beautifully crafted.
Made in my image;
You're an afterimage.

The Conceptual Circus

His soul is leaving his body now;
This was definitely a fine achievement.
How grand it is to be high.
More corpses for the catacomb.
The supreme vision in my mind's eye.
Those beneath will never understand.

If I tell you what you want to hear;
Will that make you change your mind?
You were speaking metaphorically;
Now towards talking you're disinclined.

If you were invited would you go;
Or would you just stay home?
Frisky the Clown has a new act for the kids;
He smothers them using foam.

Continuing to yearn for and willing;
The stimulation of a drug.
The circus is conceptual.
What a striking effect.
It's so effectual.
The circus' proprietor is gradually losing his mind.

The Conceptual Circus is not subject to remembrance;
But that's because it's so good.
The somatesthesia it produces is memorable.
You could join me if you would.

Those who only look on will never understand;
Why it is he can never part.
By way of reasoning philosophically;
He knew their motives from the start.

He thinks he's leaving his body now;
What a satisfactory achievement.
It's satisfying to expand.
Such things are gratifying.
Products in high demand.
An origination stemming from both cause and effect.

Throw your cautions to the wind;
It's a part of the art.
Put aside your well-being for what stimulates;
There is beauty in being torn apart.

What has happened here?
The circus' operator can be most severe.
If I tell you;
Will that change your frequency?
Will it alter your point of view?
Those who look on will never understand.

Those with selective vision will never see;
Why it is he can never dispense with.
Offering a particular type of clarity;
That's the Conceptual Circus' pith.

Burning Ants

Greet the one you love.
Massage the paper dove.
Ignore the criticisms that you've heard;
The envious have been deterred.

Eyes dilate;
Good luck with walking straight.
Staying in a trance;
Plus, the pleasure of burning ants.
What a magnificent theme.
What a splendid dream.
A neutron star.

Once an injured slave;
Now he dreams about the grave.
Where the acrimonious dwell;
It's obvious, but it's hard to tell.

Incubate.
Record the development rate.
Keep it warm to mature.
There's warmth in making sure.
She's held in high esteem.
She's the ultimate dream.
A neutron star.

To die young, or to die late.
Lay down in comfort across the grate.
The drifter has brought you here.
It's smooth, yet so severe.

Titillate.
Spasmodic movements take.
Get past it, if you please;
It puts my mind at ease.
It's a magnificent theme.
It's such a vibrant dream.
A neutron star.

Secretive Substitution

So many teachings;
With multiple meanings.
Swallow your doctrines.
Changeling adoptions.

Know your own placement;
You're the replacement.
Carry your fother;
Exchanged for another.

They'll love you more than I do.
More twisted than a corkscrew.
They love you more than I do.
The fleshiest part to cut through.

The man he endorses.
The changing of courses.
I have felt.
I have dealt.

The movement of horses;
They're running their courses.
Their behavioral adaptions.
Your use of contraptions.

They'll love you more than I can.
Shorten your own lifespan.
They love you more than I can;
After all, you're less than.

Oh, what a pity;
Interchanged for something pretty.
Having other options.
Changeling adoptions.

Exultantly elated.
Feelings unreciprocated.
Periodical screenings.
A multitude of meanings.

They'll care for you more than I will.
The lessons that they'll instill.
They'll be softer with than I will.
Shut your mouth and stay still.

An unstated agreement.
A non-mutual achievement.
There are motions in movement;
Where there's room for improvement.

The progression of horses;
They're citing their sources.
A functional enhancement.
Making strides with advancement.

A transference of ownership.
Superb one-upmanship.
A nonreciprocal kinship.
You have a gift to unrip.

Ebola

A new strain of Ebola;
Effecting non-human primates and humans.
Mental images;
The idola.
It's spreading among humans.
The virus is seething.
He is bleeding.

A new strain of Ebola;
Affecting primates, such as humans.
Spectral images;
The idola.
Non-human primates and humans.
Internal seeding.
Generating and breeding.

We know the origins;
But the destination is unclear.
It's stronger,
It's more potent now;
We're making it better each year.
A bioweapon facility.
Bow to my ability.

What the procedure will involve;
Cutting humans is human.
The apes are continuing to evolve;
Their behavior's inhuman.
Internal bleeding.
The virus is succeeding.

Snug Rooster

Snug Rooster;
I'm comfortably unwell.
He always lies alone.
Let his temperature swell.

He's now moving;
How can you tell?
He's handling all matters.
Let his temperament dwell.

Snug Rooster;
You're so all alone.
You're testing my patience;
When using that kind of tone.

In-depth.
In-depth and severe.
Why don't you go?
There's no safety here.

You did it;
You made me inspired.
You have only yourself to blame for what has transpired.

In waiting;
Too impatient to try.
Taking in what it offers;
While waiting to die.

I'm sweating.
I'll never be dry.
The more that you do it, the sooner you will die.

Somewhat grateful;
Is that enough?
Some people sleep in,
While others sleep on a surface that's rough.

I did it;
Look at what has transpired.
The deeper I drove the nails, the more he perspired.

Snug Rooster;
Wipe off that smile.
That cloud that you're riding on;
It only lasts for a while.

Snug Rooster;
You've lived great as of late.
Just as they've prosperously blown you up;
At the same rate, they'll deflate.

You'll live;
But just for a while.
You're a number to me;
Another log on the pile.

The Falling Acrobat

The beauty of deteriorating the self.
I always party all by myself.
I don't have faith in you, or your's.
You make what's dull;
You're total bores.

Whatever it is you have they want.
The dream of being skeletal, as well as, gaunt.
Your own interest is your concern.
Identifying relevance to discern.

Eliminate the self.
Eliminate yourself.
Being deserving of what you've been dealt;
I made sure you felt.

I cannot make up my mind.
A strong disinterest;
I'm disinclined.
An unwillingness to deal with that.
Awaiting the fall of the acrobat.

Provide for me an answer that's more correct.
Send me a message that's more direct.
No possibility of a rebut.
A pressurized binding inside my gut.

Damaging the self.
Doing damage to the self.
You're deserving of what you have been dealt.
I've enjoyed what I've felt.

Citizen Model

Cigarette burns on my fingers.
He's the champion of the solo game.
Reluctantly he lingers.
I have my enemies memorized by name.

It's alright.
It's not alright.
It's okay.
I'm not okay.

Misery loves company.
You don't want it to ride too smooth.
Go ahead and accompany.
Rubbing alcohol does soothe.

Things are swell;
But not so well.
Things are tight;
Yet not all's right.

What is well?
You cannot tell.
You have no choice.
You have no voice.

He has nothing to do.
He is best at the solo game.
He is bored with nothing to do.
Everything just stays the same.

Now he has too much to do;
They chose to interfere.
They had a lot to do with it;
The imaginary things you fear.

Citizen Model;
Choose to fondle.
Citizen Model;
Go full-throttle.

The Sudden Appearance of Planet 17

How does it seem?
Do twelve per diem.
Look at it now, and wait for the other to appear.
A color scheme;
Within the gleam.
I see it now,
It's opening a new frontier;
Welcoming research to all it has found.
It's in the sky, and we're on the ground.

Sarcophile;
Do wonder how.
Counterclockwise in constant rotation.
Don't disavow;
It's in the here and now.
It is showing itself.
It's the new member planet;
Inviting study to all who have found.
It drifts up above, while we are earthbound.

Are its resources rife;
To sustain life?
We think so, but we don't know for sure.
Is there water there?
What's in the air?
It's something relatively toxic, but oh it's oh so pure.
Its circumference is larger than ours.
It has many moons.
It alters the stars.

It's made its presence clear;
Appearing to us here.
They're trying to make contact using some form of communication.
A viewing eye;
From within the sky.
The surface is purple;
It's darker than Mars.
It has many rings.
It has craters for scars.

Flor Marina's Discovery of New Evidence

Come now;
Let's celebrate,
The fact it's not a holiday.
And did you hear about Flor Marina's new evidence?

An example of how the burden weighs.
Not that much was lost or gained,
But at least she found some new sort of confidence.

The ingredient of fluoride.
Black rot is glorified.
He collected all eight;
Despite the fact, he's always been a cheapskate.

Skating down the slippery slope;
His skin is coated with revertible soap.
She prefers her days alone;
Social status is overblown.

Come now;
Let's celebrate,
After all, it's not a holiday.
Her abilities are setting a new precedent.

You'll never find what you've already found.
She has since relocated.
She now resides as a new resident.

Enigmatic story show.
Radiation exposure glow.
Origins of sour glaze.
Don't take it back; rephrase.

Flor's florescent diagram.
The agenda behind the sham.
A simulation of semblance.
Day by day resemblance.

Malice in Underland

We found malice in Underland;
Beneath the surface of thermoplastic land.
Paint thinner odors and hand-rolled cigars.
Thermosetting resins, plus the finest tars.

Philotechnical.
Highly effectual.
Biotechnical.
Make them more intellectual.

Then again, on the other hand;
I'm going to get what I demand.
A dissoluble pill is a dissolvable treat.
Don't tell me that hacksaws are obsolete.

Hands on bars.
Permanent scars.
Confined in wait.
Incubate.

Oversized infants in undersized cribs.
Thick, metal bars and rubber ducky bibs.
Pacifiers washed in dioxin rain.
Use the device;
Do not complain.

Unhealthy tissue.
Avoiding the issue.
Growing pains.
Producing more stains.

That which is negative is always in demand.
End yourself using your own hand.
What was in store, they did not tell her.
Let's see if he can breathe without his inhaler.

Transcendental;
He's going mental.
Far-off course.
The provider's the source.

Plugged in toasters exposed to water.
Seeking the approval of the governor's daughter.
The pelting of the much-deserved lashes.
Pile up their remains, then turn them to ashes.

Sitting stiff.
Lying tall.
It's finally here;
The final curtain call.

Make them big.
Slice them up small.
Use your scissors;
Answer the call.

A rigid arm.
A stiffened hand.
Spread the malice;
Malice upon this land.

New Provisions for the Just

Who is with and who is without?
Your story is always the same.
There are new provisions for the just;
For those who feel so much shame.
I should have been more prompt and expeditious.
Arriving then is fair.
I should give her more than I'm providing.
A past and current interior tear.

It's not on purpose, but it's my fault.
Such a purpose;
Please, exult.
Exhilarate then design a higher rank.

Status in regard to wealth;
Is nothing unless it matters to you.
A copious abundance of poor health;
I want them to want it too.
Looking forward to her wrath and rapture;
I sat in the dry.
Desperately trying to recapture;
Her I must mollify.

On purpose and purposeful;
I know.
The ultimate purpose;
Follow.
Conceive and then contrive a higher rank.

Sent out to pasture and hung out to dry;
Isn't that such a shame?
Hold me to a higher standard;
Place upon me the blame.
I'm grateful for what you have encouraged;
I sweat you more every day.
They'll soon drop, don't be discouraged.
To their knees they'll drop, then they'll lay.

You did it on purpose;
Your fault.
So quickly she closed it;
Her vault.
I had it all planned out, but now it's in the tank.

Chromosomal Abnormalities

There are changes coming now.
Are you ready for changes?
She's giving birth to it now.
He is missing phalanges.
The plant's leaking radiation.
Enjoy your mutation.

Recognizable development;
The primordium of the tissue.
There's something wrong with his development;
A primordial issue.
Useful uranium;
It's enlarged his cranium.

Load them in the crematorium;
Counting makes it even more fun.
We've removed both of his legs;
There's no way that he can run.
Radioactivity.
Do you want to die with me?

No clear identity.
No plan, nor schema.
You're losing hair and body weight.
Others swell from edema.
Three-eyed fish in the sea.
What the hell has happened to me?

There are changes coming now.
Are you ready for changes?
She's giving birth to it now.
He's missing phalanges.
The plant's leaking radiation.
Enjoy your mutation.

Let's go find the ones that are at fault.
It was like that from the onset.
Stick around for the final result.
I'm numb, but not dead yet.
Cancer of the thyroid.
Dancing on a spheroid.

Swelling from edema.
Breathing air causes emphysema.
Free lymphedema;
Courtesy of Fukushima.

The Refusal Bed

Hurt by the refusal bed;
There is no way that I can rest my head.
It's affecting me inside;
The way that you denied.

An impact of the refusal bed;
Is that I remember every word you said.
Try not to be upset;
It's advantageous to stay saddened yet.

So much for what lies ahead;
His hypertension is all, but dead.
What portion will you share;
If there's nothing there?

Dying in the refusal bed.
It's no wonder that he lost his head.
He wanted his revenge;
To come after the binge.

Left cold like heart disease;
With but a single, identified cause.
Pressure and no kind of ease.
Another faux pas.

Everyone's liveness is tapering.
Exactly which of us is she favoring?
To her, I'm more inclined to submit;
To be subservient.

She denies what she wants.
Fully conceal it;
Do ensconce.
I'm willing to commit.
Make us closely knit.

Puppeteer and Marionette

Being controlled like a marionette.
All of the results of motion have not been seen yet.
The puppeteer is conducting all of his schemes.
The recidivist may exist, but she's not what she seems.

Watching the show.
Pulling the strings.
Controlling the flow.
See what it brings.

Being regimented like a marionette.
Disturbing the balance to further upset.
Illogically drawn to a logical conclusion.
You should be proud of every contusion.

The ringing ear;
It rings so true.
You should embrace it;
My power over you.

Creating the show.
Conducting the strings.
Killing them slowly;
And the pleasure it brings.

To be managed like a well-trained puppet.
Panic induced vomiting into a bucket.
You should admire the sizable amount.
Upon my wall of species your head I'll mount.

Playing controller.
Playing God.
This is how you get off;
Hear them applaud.

Manipulate.
Control the condition.
Do it again;
We love repetition.

Burning Bridges and Leaving Whelps

I.
I guess.
I guess I've burnt those bridges.
Who?
They have left.
They left everything just as it was.

Help;
It left a welt.
He's so happy on his merry way.
The passive voice.
Don't rejoice.
Savor your misery; that's what I say.

They?
They went left.
They left everything the way it was.
Comment;
That's what I meant.
They hated everything the way it was.

Die.
Just die.
I hated everything about who he was.
Resent;
That's what she meant.
I don't remember exactly when it was.

No restrictions.
No laws.
Repetitive mistruths were a significant cause.
Being shiny;
It's smooth.
She can still be wonderful with character flaws.

Mandatory Conditioning

Inject me as I utter.
Caress me with it as I flutter.
Internal sense.
External favors.
They do not ask you to sign waivers.
The willingness of destructive devotion.
I set the adverse into motion.
The things I do.
The ones I've done.
My completion has no doubt begun.

Inject me,
I've not fallen.
Detect me,
Though I am sullen.
Things come to the one that savors.
I will save her if she wavers.
A willingness of great devotion.
Onward stepping;
Moving forward in motion.

The undercurrents.
The undertows.
Let's make examples of those who owe.
A period of judgment.
The phase of remotion.
Deeper depths.
An improved potion.
Hides preserved by using lotion.
Onward steps;
Falling forward into the ocean.

Cure me of this mental ailment.
A reduction.
A curtailment.
Shorten this episode of panic.
The panic phase is galvanic.
Pure in passion.
Pure in emotion.
Forgive me for the preconceived notion.
Be punctilious.
Bring your comfort.
Put an end to my reoccurring discomfort.

A place to lay,
My heart's chambers.
A place to stay,
A room for tamers.
Domesticize the human you're training.
Make it tractable.
Be with it constraining.
Commitment to the ultimate purpose.
You can make it multipurpose.
Calculations and numerical scheming.
Remove the skin from a human being.

Avoid careful behavior.
Keep from overcareful behavior.
Be your own oppressor and enslaver.
Eliminate those who do not favor.

Be quixotical;
Think quixotically.
Be fanatical;
Make them run frantically.

Perfect for Grooming

I can't believe that this has transpired.
Once full of energy;
Now so tired.
Come and let me touch you.
Sense the embracement from my hands.
Stop squirming,
Let me groom you.
Meet my expectations.
Meet my demands.

The caretaker who was careless never cared about you.
Stiffly posturing;
Stiff like a statue.
Aiding your development;
I'm the only person that understands.
They're peremptory;
Obey all of my commands.

I don't remember exactly when, or what transpired.
Once vibrant with vitality;
Now nearly expired.
Let me feel you.
Interpret the language from my hands.
You need caressing.
Autocratic types of plans.

No memory of the incident, or how it transpired.
Calmness comes even less;
When you are wired.
Provide me with some comfort.
I like that you are macilent.
Enter to usher.
Comfort can be violent.

I want you to have more of an understanding.
There are more things to learn during your expanding.
Be obsessive.
Let's depart from this place.
Be aggressive.
Run your nails smoothly down my face.

Sudden departure.
Unified departure.
Innocently unassuming;
Perfect for grooming.

Lactose Tolerant

Bad luck and serendipity.
No fruits, yet fruit to bear.
Exaggerated grinning all along.
Fine whines and fine fragility.
Talk to it when nobody's there.
Exercising the root causes it to prolong.

Ongoing and informational;
Communication with oneself.
The feedback was placed within your tone.
Ongoing and confrontational;
Responses to oneself.
Make her hear it, and make it known.

Presentiate.
Make it known.
The reproduction of the clone.
Progressing well;
The cancer's lean.
The complexity of what is labyrinthine.

Presentiate.
Make it known.
Why are they hiding what should be shown?
The process went well,
It's so benign;
Pay homage to the wet nurses' wine.

No fortune, yet serendipity.
Discovered, but still concealed.
One will live, yet one will die alone.
Nose growth with fine fertility.
He grins wider when he lies.
Himself personally,
He does prise.

Keep it coming;
Do not wean.
Liquid silk is fresh and clean.
Processing well,
The lifeline stands;
That which is produced by mammary glands.

Distribute;
Do not wean.
It's nature's beacon.
It's nature's spring.
Absorbing well, the lifeline stands.
Nourishment from the mammary glands.

A Prodigy of Prosody

Apostasy;
No apology.
Causes and views are in opposition now.
You're the key;
Walk far with me.
She's the embodiment of beauty; the decipherable way how.

Reinvent;
To what extent?
You have to give yourself if you wish to proceed.
Sign on the line if you want to succeed.

The morphology.
An anthology;
Memorize the passages I've chosen for you.
A prodigy;
Of prosody.
Within the meadow lies oranges, in addition to, meadow rue.

Circumvent;
With ill intent.
Soon the patron will surely recede.
They only come back to get what they need.

Her epiphany.
An antiphony.
Passing from one state to another.
We will do just as we agreed.
An illuminating rest.
It's time to exceed.

Transfixion

It's form;
It's not the norm.
Introduce it to your bloodstream;
Make your insides warm.

Within;
So without.
Give it some flame;
Show them what it's about.

I'm out;
Let me on in.
Let me inside you;
Welcome the comfort of sin.

Believe;
Only what you perceive.
Recognize the balance;
I have to get what I need.

Begin;
Stain your insides.
Hold it deep within.
Look at what it provides.

Butchered;
Slain like a calm pig.
The more that you like it,
The bigger hole you will dig.

The host;
He's fully engrossed.
Transfixed by what's inside him,
And what he hates most.

Check-in;
Before you check out.
Pick up a gun;
Show them what it's about.

Listen;
I'm hearing a voice.
Tempting tides.
A maker making a choice.

Malformed Fetus

He thought a lot about death's inducement.
Stimulation addicts don't worry about health improvement.
I'm going to lock my door, so I can circumvent.
I said exactly what I meant.

Fallopian tubes and late-term infants.
Her amniotic sac chose to burst in this instance.
Lean back really far for postural positioning.
You've become dependent from a lifetime of conditioning.

Physical impairment.
He doesn't want you to see.
Health impairments.
He doesn't want to be.

Waiting with anxiety and anticipation.
I'm waiting impatiently for my sedation.
The ongoing view is pessimistic.
My sacrificing of him was ritualistic.

He kept it hidden.
It's what they couldn't see.
He never wanted.
He never wanted to be.

A permanent impairment.
His disabilities.
He's sought care;
In various facilities.

She was in misery, because of her gestation.
She felt the opposite of anticipation.
I really think that he'd like to be us.
Her uterus contains another developing, malformed fetus.

Quicklime

Lay down all of your will.
Self-construct to destruct.
Contaminate it after you distill.
Induct then obstruct.
Come on my trustee;
Tell me that you're here with me.

On the sign was a logogram.
There's a symbol for that word.
From her tongue came an epigram;
It was the debut that you heard.
The saying is with me.
Sweating will distill me.

The mender didn't repair it well;
He mostly just collects utensils.
The fixer has a hunger to quell;
He carries with him some stencils.
Read it all, not just the extract.
You subtract and detract.

Put him up here upon the slab.
Our nurturance will be a blessing.
There's room here in our research lab.
The situation is pressing.
His breathing's becoming murmurous;
That's better than stertorous.

She's safer within our hands;
Once before we succeeded.
Adhere to all of our demands;
Your cooperation is needed.
It's easier to manage when it's sprayed.
Please, don't let her be spayed.

Do it in a shorter frame of time;
Cover them with quicklime.
Moving faster would be a plus;
But she still won't forgive us.
Come to cum with me.
Someone, please kill me.

Short-Term Thrill

I said;
Won't you heal my head?
I don't need your advice;
I need the substance instead.

It's within;
The mission's complete.
The short-term thrill is something you can buy on the street.

Don't;
You know that he won't.
He's never going to try.
Let them stay where they lie.

Severe;
So cavalier.
Haughty disregard for the ones that are here.

The situation;
The situation then.
Store him as you would an object.
Keep him within his bin.

The subject.
The subject's near.
No assistance for you;
Why did you come here?

Suffer.
Suffer for your art.
The most compelling of things;
They come from the pain in your heart.

I liked it;
I liked the way it bled.
Do not interrupt;
My disease needs to be fed.

The matter;
The matter at hand.
Solve it with a chainsaw;
Make yourself grand.

You can suffer.
No, I don't care;
But I promise you,
I'll help you get there.

A Gradual Plunging

Not receiving what she's after;
She hasn't been cared for properly.
Unhappily ever after;
She always speaks so somberly.

Don't look now.
Conceal your eyes.
Maintain your sight.
She firmly defies.
She accepts her impecuniousness.
Hardship with lies;
Expect nothing less.

Increasingly colder;
It presents itself in a challenging way.
Directly addressing the beholder;
She believes everything you say.

Without obtaining what she wanted;
Disappointment rests at her core.
His growth has been stunted;
Raising positivity like never before.

Being unaware;
She doesn't care.
Look at all;
There's nothing there.
She never knew exactly what you meant.
The things they promised;
They haven't sent.

Not getting what was needed;
She has resorted to displeasing acts.
Lamenting as she conceded;
In her existence, they are just the facts.

Clean it now;
To later clean again.
Do begrime;
Just like back then.
Now she knows exactly just what you meant.
Her optimism's subsided;
Downward descent.

Artificially Flavored Carpet

Life is fucking swell;
As if you couldn't tell.
Life is bittersweet;
Especially when you have meat.

I guess it's nothing new;
Boredom and nothing to do.
Paranoia from multiple calls.
Peeling paint from my bedroom walls.

Life is kind of real;
Especially when you don't heal.
The others think you're great;
For you, I have only hate.

The days are exactly the same;
Who am I to blame?
I guess I'll blame the one;
Who holds the sign of his son.

She really loves handbags;
And she'll only hang out with fags.
Not to be harassed;
She's deleted her past.

I can remember well;
The things you couldn't tell.
You were too stupid to know.
You've nothing clever to show.

What made the pendulum stop?
Was it a sonic boom or pop?
Randy's building a bomb;
Stored on a CD-ROM.

Artificially flavored carpet.
A better experience for Margaret.
She wallows around on the floor;
When there's a steady knock at the door.

Jan the Janitor

Jan the janitor;
That's her title.
Afraid to face it?
Push brooms are vital.

She really hurts tonight;
But that's how it will be.
She's all alone, just like me at night;
What a facsimile.

Scrub the toilets.
Are you having fun?
Stick it inside your mouth;
The barrel of the gun.

Jan the janitor;
Your mission's vital.
You need to clean up;
Before the recital.

Jan always hurts at night.
Refuse to agree.
She doesn't even try anymore.
What else can she be?

How is your day so far?
Are you maintaining your breathing?
What an uninteresting job.
Permanent teething.

A dead-end job with no end in sight;
She's accepted her destiny.
The shine produced by mopping;
What a highlight.
Her manifesting predestiny.

Population Management

Abort all implementations; the patient's unstable.
He's paranoid, but he sure is able.
He carries a great deal of weight in his heart.
Mix the two substances; that's a hell of a start.

When he saw heaven he witnessed a slaughter.
He was baptized by his pubescent daughter.
I'm full of joy; where is my gun?
Blow your head off to be a chosen one.

The concept.
The gestation.
It's been implemented;
Depopulation.

Look at my carrot; it's beta-carotene.
Recover to give more to your favorite acarine.
Facts came from unwarranted suspicion.
Please resume the lithotomy position.

Do with me what you must.
You have grown and reaped my distrust.
The feces he was fed before he was weaned;
It resulted in his complexion being yellow-tinged.

Reprogram.
Read the program.
An elaborate operation.
The culmination.

Willow's Effectivity

Beauty within the monster;
A monster within the beauty.
Hurt me so.
Damage me.
I intuitively know.
Invariably arriving here.
Instinctively knowing makes it more severe.

She was merciless to the flame;
That's why she put it out.
She always selected to win the game;
Because that's what her game's about.

The beauty within a monster;
A monster within the beauty.
Destroy me so.
Just like the drooping tree;
They named you Willow.
You hang your head down;
Though you are divine.

She was unmerciful to what was alive;
Unsentimental and pitiless.
Yearning for even more of what you deprive;
We were better left didymous.

The exhilaration offered by the pillow.
As is the weeping trees';
Your name is Willow.
Approaches does the dawn.
No rest for the occupied.
Insomniacs carry on.
Continue on through the tribulations of trials.

Her beauty willing will still exist;
Full with bountifulness.
Fully enamored I do persist;
She should expect nothing less.

Freakshow Martyr

Wait in line.
Stand by on standby.
The carnival has come to town.
The clown has a really big frown.

Carnival freak boy;
The subject.
No empathy.
No empathy placed upon.
Carnival freak boy;
The product.
Bad conduct.
The lambasting carries on.

Do what you do best.
No problem.
His problems.
No fosterage received.
Freakshow martyr;
So ugly,
So stupid;
He's bewildered and bereaved.

He doesn't comprehend.
No grasp.
No thought.
What you said was misconceived.
There's no evidence.
No evidence.
Not proven;
He denies what he once believed.

No substantiation.
No proof,
Nor validity.
Just continue to ramble on.
All you say is based on false claims.
His own picture is what he frames.

It can't be;
The impossible's not possible.
He can not be real.
Why does he stay so still?

There's no gravitation.
They're keeping their distance.
They're staying away from where he is.
They don't know it.
Just hide it,
Don't show it.
They're exactly what he is.

Freakshow martyr;
Long fangs with tartar.
Infestations upon.
The carnival must go on.

Freakshow martyr;
When he's irritable he's tarter.
Let his complaints go unheard.
Ignore his every pleading word.

Consummate Consumption

He's out.
He's out of control.
He knows why he needs it;
It makes him feel whole.

Extol.
It's taking a toll.
He knows why he needs it;
It soothes his body and soul.

Extol.
Existence in a bowl.
He doesn't really care;
No need to console.

The pit.
The same old shit.
Owning various reasons;
He's not afraid to commit.

Searching;
Seeking what isn't there.
He swears he's semisolid;
Being so easy to tear.

It's primal;
His fundamental practice.
With no wet-nurse to suckle;
He's described as agalactous.

To succumb.
To be inundated.
With overwhelming factors;
Your body is weighted.

Compound;
The subjects have mated.
Train their progeny well;
Until domesticated.

Xanax

Staying on all the right tracks.
Staying on Xanax.
Nicotine, vascular ride.
Carbon monoxide.
It's effortless to pick up an axe.
Extra effort to relax.

Try this pill, it's something new;
It might make you all better.
It's been ignored like a parvenu;
Let's make it a pacesetter.
Nicotine, vascular ride.
Black tar on the inside.

Don't concern yourself, it's just the facts.
Take all of your Xanax.
It's another sedative that you know.
Do an upper;
Do blow.
It's a determinant.
Memory loss isn't permanent.

Go ahead and combine the two;
It makes it all the better.
I'm a little less anxious with you.
I'll send a crank letter.
Dear benzodiazepine;
Cleanse me like hexachlorophene.

It's something that can be taken in;
A temporary solution.
It works quickly when it's within;
A speedy distribution.
A personal discovery;
From which there's no recovery.

Paresthesia

Stuck within a mental state.
Nobody cares so don't be late.
Go ahead; take this avenue.
Your complexion is changing hue.

She told me her anecdote.
They still haven't found an antidote.
Within there lies the best remedy;
Keep this just for you and me.

Striving for higher elevations;
More heightened interest and sensations.
Higher degrees of paresthesia.
Epistaxis and peripeteia.

Just because you make others mad;
Doesn't mean you should change your attitude.
From the condition of being sad;
Comes not caring, with, no sense of gratitude.

A sense of what will feel the best.
They've all gathered here just to infest.
Historically they've done it on many occasions before;
Leaving you drained and wanting more.

Perform Beautifully, Precious

Oh what a tragedy;
The trait of frequent apathy.
No enthusiasm.
An absence of enthusiasm.
I'm pulling your strings now, Precious;
For the first act has begun.

Inner colors.
Inward coloring.
You did disseminate.
Innards colored.
Inner coloring.
You didn't remunerate.

Oh, what a tragedy.
The abbot of the abbacy.
It's unreal.
Focused on an unreality;
Tell them how you really feel.
Does it help you to better understand?

They did not compensate;
Even though they promised they would.
Continue to perform beautifully;
Show them that they're no good.

Get a hold of yourself, Precious;
They do expect a showing.
You're not allowed to cry.
You've been well worth knowing.
Those who live are meant to die.
Step outside of the box to say your goodbye.

Display all that lies inside;
Even if it's all black.
Audiences may leave due to circumstance;
But eventually, they'll come back.

Perform for us, Precious;
We need you to refresh us.
Oh, how divine.
The performance isn't over,
Give us another line;
Another line before you retreat.

Leave it all upon the stage;
Don't give in to conformity.
Watch them as they turn another page;
My precious abnormity.

Butter Messiah

Running quickly from a fear of sobriety.
Commit yourself to impropriety.
Don't spit it out just because it's insipid.
An offering of protein, plus, a lot of lipids.

Butter Messiah;
We're talking to you.
Give us carbohydrates.
Give us something to do.

Butter Messiah;
We love you.
Give us a reason.
Give us someone to do.

Look at David; he's born again.
He likes to jump around inside his pen.
He has been planning his great escape.
The resurrection of the devotee ape.

Evolution comes in many forms.
He'll love him more when he conforms.
A spawn of the world's giant clit.
Animal feces is valuable shit.

Butter Messiah;
Come to me.
Soak my bread;
Then leave me be.

Let the lipids accumulate.
Let them accrue.
It's adipose.
It's fatty tissue.

One of his creatures was better than the other.
He decided to offer up his premature brother.
There is new hope for the common pariah.
Here comes the deliverer;
The Butter Messiah.

Watch them weep as they opine.
I am more appreciative when I whine.
A steady recurrence without relief;
The reoccurring unifier in my motif.

Butter Messiah;
Give me a sign.
Grant me excrement.
The tumor isn't benign.

Provide me with death.
Show me some signs.
Give me ordure.
Provide me with whines.

The Bathroom Party Scene

Come and party inside of the bathroom.
Come to party just like we do.
Stems and bowls burn up your lighters;
That's why I always carry two.

Ventilation and smoke-stained mirrors;
Step back and close the window too.
Every so often someone will collapse;
If you're really lucky then you will too.

Mix your hell with what's serene.
Stay unclean in the restroom scene.

Light it up inside of the bathroom.
As a teen, I began to groom.
Sit on the edge of or lie in the tub;
Remember that it can be a toilet too.

Taking part and participation;
Slowly dying is something to do.
Nicotine stains on the walls of the bathroom.
Today's your lucky day; lucky you.

Cigarette burns on all of my fingers.
They sell a lot on Florida Street.
A fast pace and repeated leaving.
Pharmaceuticals make it complete.

You can get sick from dirty needles;
Hepatitis B and C.
You can get sick from blood transfusions.
I'm energetic like I have H.I.V.

There's no limit to what you can bring.
Stay unclean in the bathroom scene.

Loathing

The sun never shines;
At least not for me.
That's somewhat realistic;
At least to a certain degree.
Melancholy, and all of the things that you've had.
It's a bit gloomy;
It's not so bad.
Consistent complaining;
Because being consistent is best.
I crave her attention;
While ignoring the rest.

Someday I'll return there;
Someday I guess.
Their positive, good fortune;
Put me to the test.
Focus on the things that you've never had.
I like that you're stupid.
I hope you feel bad.
Don't say goodbye;
Unless you promise to leave.
You are an annoyance.
Your flesh I will cleave.

They parted ways;
Only to be coalesced.
I'm very manic;
That's why I can't rest.
Melancholy is something that we should all have.
Maybe I enjoy it.
Maybe I'm glad.
Highly diluted;
You've become less severe.
The statement you made;
It was clearly unclear.

Your normalcy kills me;
Being unoriginal at best.
Since your condition has worsened;
I'm feeling blessed.
Good things shall come to all the people that take.
That must be just.
Look at them slake.

Epinephrine Exudation

Epinephrine secretion as a result of stress.
You should sleep where I make my mess.
Your performance is not meeting all of the requirements.
Premature deaths equal early retirements.

It starts in moderation, but then you'll need more;
To obtain the feeling that you felt before.
You have to fill that if you want to feel this.
If you ever leave it behind it will be sorely missed.

Further up;
Look what I've found.
The calling is constant.
The substance is compound.

The human body is biodegradable.
You are controlled because you are persuadable.
You have to do that if you want to do this.
He is someone they will not miss.

A certain amount of ease due to my supply.
You could experience it too, but you don't try.
You have to do this if you want to feel that.
Make way for another inner spat.

The inner core.
The inner ear.
What is that sound?
What do I hear?

Higher up;
Yet totally downed.
A yearning that's constant.
A substance that's compound.

Geodon

One time on some Geodon;
I thought I lived inside of a TV.
Your happy days were long and now gone.
I must have contracted some T.B.

They were good times;
That's what they say.
There were good times;
But not today.

Those were good times;
That's what they say.
There were good times;
But they've gone away.

This one time I thought I was talking to God;
But then I made it out of the coma.
Separate, but dependent parts.
Problems in the psyche and soma.

You don't understand a word I say;
But you should find it to be self-explanatory.
Too manic and volcanic to lay.
Some I've heard keep their tactics dilatory.

Are they coming?
No, not today.
Will you find it?
Maybe someday.

Did you see it?
It was something.
Did you see them?
They were thumping.

Come tell me something I already know;
That's what most have done historically.
I don't need any direction from you;
I was just talking about being lost metaphorically.

A steady supply of options here.
I'm really driven by words of ridicule.
Manipulate then commandeer.
I'm busy doing something that'll really cure.

Better moments;
That's when they stray.
Soak and foment.
What did I say?

Better moments;
Have them your way.
There was one time;
But today's gray.

Open wounds can be filled with salt;
It's more pleasurable if the wounds are deeper.
Don't look at me; I'm not at fault.
I chose them because they were much cheaper.

She does well on roller skates;
I think that's why she rolls with positive fortune.
I cannot skate, but I'm never late.
What happened was blown out of proportion.

Bird-Scarer

Scarecrow;
You allowed them to grow.
A farmer made you;
I guess he knew how to sew.

Scarecrow;
You guard what they grow.
The herder's herding sheep;
I guess we do what we know.

Bird-scarer;
You're a fine effigy.
Can you see who's around you?
Can you see them like me?

Strawman;
You're a specter to show.
You came to be so long ago.

Scarecrow;
They stuffed you with straw.
Do you hurt like you're real?
Does the mast make you raw?

And afterward, they assembled a golden fence.
He thinks of things that simply don't make sense.
Occupying even during instances of rain;
He watches the field as he admires the grain.

Another emergence of growth is about to commence.
His thoughts are involved with mostly the present tense.
Occupied during instances of both sun and rain;
He hangs on his pole while receiving pleasure from pain.

Transfiguration

I would expect nothing less.
Carry your sword, my prophetess.
Obstinate contumacy training.
Find the objective that is more draining.
More strenuous tasks will make you grow.
Pain upon you I bestow.
I'll take it all and nothing less.
I claim it back;
I repossess.

Tip the scale;
Turn it over.
Mark the unused;
What's leftover.
The main part no longer exists;
Despite the reduction, it persists.
Continued movement;
A quest for traction.
An opposite and negative reaction.

Hex induced metamorphosis;
Reoccur once again for us.
Physically and internally changing.
The process of rearranging.
The alteration was so fitting.
Now they're pausing;
They're intermitting.
In reaffirming the causation;
Keep kempt, and maintain your original explanation.

Wear our serpent, prophetess;
Prior to you was profitless.
The soil was sown with no reaping.
Tear our hearts out for your keeping.
Beyond the boundaries of what is permitted.
Reward me for the sins I've committed.
My acts were bold;
Caress my flesh.
I give it all and nothing less.

The facsimile will shudder.
Express what it is I utter.
Amidst psychos and others.
Among psychos and others.

Live with vigor;
Efficiently transfigure.
Disfigure;
Change his figure.
Make it so;
Mark the torso.
Undergo;
Nock the torso.
Let it grow;
Open the torso.
Let him know;
Carve the torso.

Escapism

I'm really glad that you brought it here;
My stomach muscles will tighten.
There's a ringing in my inner ear.
Hold it in to heighten.
There's not enough to be generous.
I choose to be venomous.

What is exactly happening here?
Personal punishment is so severe.
It is never going to cease.
Hold it in to increase.
Escaping certain aspects is a must.
All of you I so distrust.

I'm really happy we have it here;
It's a major improvement.
You need to do it every day of the year.
Suffering from a lack of movement.
Finishing well is a personal must.
In all of you, I distrust.

I'm really glad I bought it here;
It adds something to each moment.
The final intake will soon be here;
Give me a moment.
Once was deaf, but now I see.
What the hell just happened to me?

More was done that interval;
Though it was a short duration.
In a state that is hibernal;
Metabolic hibernation.
Always come bearing gifts;
I particularly like the way it lifts.

A Codependent Romance

Why do you have to make it more;
More of a difficult situation?
You should more greatly appreciate my infatuation.
We need to make some changes.
We need to improve.
Let's handle this with care, and in an efficient way.

I remember well;
When normalcy was enough.
Add an ingredient;
Stir it with your spoon.
No quantity is excessive, nor will it qualify as enough.
It could not have happened in any higher form.

Don't say goodnight;
It's not slight.
I'm never going to sleep again.
The drug's deployed.
I'm paranoid.
Will I ever wake again?

Rely upon me; as I rely on you.
Nurturance with warming smoothness;
Render it as you do.
Codependency;
Dependance upon you.
This could not have occurred in any greater form.

Something has happened to lead us to this point.
Find commonality within my solace;
Never to disjoint.
Be sure to follow me.
Be sure to ignore there.
Everyone needs at least one outing;
A one outing affair.

Don't say good night.
We're doing it right.
Virtues will come from it.
The way I feed.
The way I need.
I can confide in it.

Nighty night;
I've got more.
I guess it's time to sleep again.
Trust upon.
Carry on;
This place is for escaping in.

Some things never change;
The cohesive parts still stick together.
Chemical compounds as a means of sustenance.
Discomfort;
For comfort.
You are silent, but I hear you.
Paranoia often;
But there's just no other path.

An inorganic, powdered complexion.
Deviate to the deviant;
Engage in flexion.
Contorted and categorized.
You can make that assumption;
I'm so overly impressed.
I'm dumbfounded by your gumption;
You've been truly blessed.

Delivery.
Deliver me;
Ritualistically administered.
Transport.
Contort.
Transcendence is much preferred.

Transportation

I saw them jump from there.
Accumulation is in the air.
If you go with me, then we can go anywhere.

This is where she found a lock.
This is where I smoked in school.
If we try hard enough we can teach him to be a tool.

Birthdays with no type of cake.
Many minutes are at stake.
Experiencing anxiousness.
Eventual and calamitous.
Not your garden-variety.
Gaining notoriety.
Heterogeneity;
A unique identity.
Biowarfare caused infections.
Examinations followed by inspections.
No concern for the end results.
Use your favorite insults.

At the edge of a stool.
A healthy dose of bread and gruel.
I think he's just brave enough to be a fool.

There are too many things to do;
When living with too much care.
If you go with me then I can go anywhere.

Cult driven, mass suicides.
Holly's making new strides.
Kids, do not behave.
You are just a modern slave.
Open to interpretation.
Total brain detonation.
Personal mismanagement.
He is definitely not ambulant.
Running with an amputee.
Waiting for the apogee.
The long-awaited climactic phase.
Do I have to paraphrase?

From nuclear winter to thermal spring.
You're entitled to the engagement ring;
And if you'll try with me then, we can try anything.

Many events are happenstance;
Could you see it with a glance?
Take my hand, so that we have half a chance.

Preparations to conjugate.
Juice beyond its expiration date.
Solve the problems of the prior.
More tea for the rectifier.
She carries her best self all the time;
Crafting every moment in her prime.
Undergoing the process of scansion.
She's organic beingness expansion.
Independent, punk-poet counterculture.
An antidote to the watching vulture.
Add more complexity to optimize.
Repeat.
Reprise.

From the dead of winter to her summer attire.
Singing not with, but against the choir;
Her range is so that you cannot hear them now.

It all led to a grand event.
The very fiber of what she's meant.
We could've never experienced that had we not have went.

World Consumer

She is a total heart consumer;
And I want to be consumed by her.
Absorb the noon.
Take in the midday,
Clothes lying strewn.
It's beneficial;
It's propitious, and it is official.

Without the projection of Andrea's gifts;
What can a person do?
Never think you're beyond mass consumption;
You're a consumer too.

She's a total heart consumer.
There's a voice behind the rumor.
Interiorize what has begun.
Take in the relevant.
Internalize the one.
She's unbound;
The one I have found.

Mentally created images viewed as actual;
What else can someone do?
It's all-consuming and relevant.
You can have someone in your head too.

See what it's developed into;
The obsession within there.
To fantasize;
A retained mental moment.
A persistent mental stare.
Interior motives.
Endogenous wear.

Originating and derived from an external source;
Obtained by way of choice.
The recognization of her superfluous image.
The recognition of her voice.

Miss Ladderville

Whether it's winter or summertime she basks in the glow.
She produces sunlight.
She's the one that makes it grow.

I always know exactly where it is she goes.
Yes, I am a stalker.
I have various highs and lows.

I know precisely where she's been and what it is she chose.
Fostering invention;
While wearing splendid clothes.

The inventor of several instruments, including, rodent traps;
She likes the attention when everyone stands and claps.

She's labeled me obsessive;
But at least it shows I care.
Some people collect baseball cards;
Some of us locks of hair.

Certain citizens stand on telephone poles;
And certain others stand in wait.
Your ribs are clearly showing;
When was the last time that you ate?

Some residents are in the trees;
They're watching from over there.
They're totally perceptible;
When they're seeking cooler air.

Some days sunlight's directed on the other side of the hill.
She carries her new contraption upon the streets of Ladderville.

Wanderlust

Wondering low;
I'm wondering about you.
Are you tending to your orchard?
It's within your purview.

Wonder low;
Wandering deep below.
This is the place I'm in;
I need you to know.

Wonderless;
I wonder what's wrong with you.
Are you unaffected;
Am I askew?

A labyrinth;
The labyrinth that is you.
Maneuvering my way;
Making my way through.

Wanderlust;
A need to make my way to you.
I have your pictures.
I must pursue.

You're wondrous.
You're the individual that I look to.
I'm well aware of that;
She could have a retinue.

Curiousness;
I'm curious about you.
No matter the age it is;
It's like it's new.

Wanderlust;
I'll go where I need to.
Continuing on;
Continuing to ensue.

The Final Product

Provide me with a container to store my cells.
They're theologians because religion sells.
Lash yourself while you weep.
He owns you, therefore, your soul he'll keep.

So unassertive;
He's not determined.
His conception;
It wasn't predetermined.

Once he got the thing he wanted, he wanted another.
His parents' favorite child was his deformed brother.
That says it all, and that says something.
You will not live beyond twenty-something.

You are emotionless when you are hollow.
They were trained well; they were taught to swallow.
After being blessed by a spray paint huffer;
He graduated and became a professional snuffer.

Your design;
He's on the decline.
Appendages plucked.
Your special product.

Bring them together.
Adduct.
Similar parts combined.
The final product.

FIVE POEMS FROM EXOTIC NEUROTIC

Anorexic Santa Claus

If you refuse to go to bed;
He will remove your head.
He vomits for a cause.
Anorexic Santa Claus.

Let him come into your home.
He wants to make you foam.
Delivering pain without a pause;
Is the anorexic Santa Claus.

Gagging is contagious;
Not to mention advantageous.
Puking without a pause;
Christmas' anorexic Santa Claus.

Your repellent scent tells him you are near.
His radar tells him when you are here.
He'll hate you if you act pleasant.
If you are pleasant you will not get a present.

Pestilence within finely wrapped boxes.
I want to see you open all of your boxes.
A self-appointed representative of Christ;
He releases more waste when he's enticed.

He only gives his best toys;
To the naughtiest girls and boys.
Go ahead, and hang your stocking.
Claus will soon be knocking.

He wants to beat you;
And maybe even eat you.
Afterwards, he'll throw-up.
He's posing for a close-up.

His stomach is churning.
He's internally burning.
Genocide without a pause;
The anorexic Santa Claus.

Kaposi's Sarcoma

It's been many years since Charlie has showered.
By a rapist, he was roughly deflowered.
Born a piece of trash, he will remain the same.
Generations of incest are most likely to blame.

He wears a dress because he's a homosexual.
The frigid turnip has become hypersexual.
Charlie was placed in a nursing home.
He acquired immune deficiency syndrome.

He's such a mess.
His stature is small.
Refuse to feed him.
Don't feed him at all.

Transfusion trades;
He's learned a trade.
Spread it on purpose;
Another one laid.

Partaking in the spreading of Aids.
Sharing blood by way of needles and razor blades.
I enjoy seeing his many defections.
He has lost the ability to fight infections.

He's expecting to die from pneumonia;
Either that or Kaposi's Sarcoma.
His request was to be cremated.
Instead, for him a black casket awaited.

Infect them with;
Immune system disease.
There is no cure.
Spread and seize.

Sniff really hard;
Smell the aroma.
Charlie died;
From Kaposi's Sarcoma.

Bonnie's Destruction of the Pristine Dishes

Long live rage, as well as, tragedy.
They'll live evermore.
I am confident without your trust.
I'm glad that life is a major whore.
She has washed her spotless dishes;
But they will never dry.
She has washed her pristine wishes;
But the promises were all lies.

Long live straining and intact notions.
Some people live life only for chores.
I am confident that you will rust.
It is now time to produce the spores.
She has left the rumor vacant.
Gossip is left for thought.
She has left the tumor vacant.
She is exactly what you are not.

I created my own discontent.
Contentment is absent and far away.
Indulging in misery without consent;
I wonder what Bonnie would say?
She possesses her own opinions.
Bonnie's judgment is viewed as fair.
She should put on display her dominion.
Long live misery and despair.

Putrid Birth

The daffodils of youth are still smelling putrid.
They have grown beside my plastic, crucified cupid.
I wonder if they want to rot with me in my nest?
An unceasing pain in my pressured chest.

He was underdeveloped for his age.
His parents restrained him within their personal cage.
He was ungratefully nourished by way of container.
His umbilical cord spewed just like a complainer.

He was never washed spotless, or with good measure.
He never acquired, but he still sought pleasure.
'Eliminate me, please,' was his final thought.
I have long been prepared for the eternal rot.

There are constant clicks because the tube is feeding.
I hear constant clicks because his organs are bleeding.
Interminably will remain your absence of worth.
I'm providing putrid flowers for your putrid birth.

Pestilential Containment

How it does spread, that what is contagious.
A transmissible disease.
I must protect her from what is contagious.
My mind is not at ease.

Your containment;
Let's frame it.
Your suffering is my entertainment.
Your imprisonment;
It's for my own good.
I'm going to do this just as I should.

I must guard her from all that is disadvantageous.
Embrace all which is demonic.
Mesmerized by what is contagious.
I am pleased that his pain is chronic.

I strain.
You're contained.
Your malnourishment is well maintained.
The portrait;
It's been framed.
The portrait showing that you I've maimed.

They have discovered that the latest plague is, in fact, pneumonic.
Engage in practices that are demonic.
The physically deformed child's spiteful reply was well done and laconic.
It's comforting to know that his pain is chronic.

Wheel chair bound with no aspirations;
He has no desire to achieve.
He has run out of anticipations.
Despite death, his pain will not leave.

My whip;
Your lashing.
To tear your flesh was beautifully smashing.
It's eating you;
Your ailment.
I'm preparing a stake for your impalement.

About the Author

Kenneth Jarrett Singleton is a thirty-four-year-old poet, playwright, and author. Prior to this book of poetry, Singleton had five books published. His first book was a science-fiction/horror novel called, The Cadaver Factory. It received publication in (2004) when he was twenty years of age. His second novel, The Donner Society, was published in (2005) the same year as his first play, Angelica and Francesca. Singleton's first book of poetry, Exotic Neurotic, was released in (2016). Following, Exotic Neurotic, his second play, Nicu II and Victoria's Incestuous Romance, was released the next year. Singleton resides in the state of West Virginia.

www.ingramcontent.com/pod-product-compliance
Lightning Source LLC
Chambersburg PA
CBHW080847120626
46553CB00009B/2601